YOUNG PROFILES

Jessica Simpson

Jill C. Wheeler

ABDO Publishing Company

visit us at
www.abdopub.com

Published by ABDO Publishing Company, 4940 Viking Drive, Edina, Minnesota 55435.
Copyright © 2005 by Abdo Consulting Group, Inc. International copyrights reserved in
all countries. No part of this book may be reproduced in any form without written
permission from the publisher. The Checkerboard Library™ is a trademark and logo of
ABDO Publishing Company.

Printed in the United States.

Cover Photo: Getty Images
Interior Photos: Corbis pp. 13, 15, 19, 26, 27, 28-29, 31; Getty Images pp. 5, 7, 9, 10, 11,
        17, 21, 23, 25

Editors: Heidi M. Dahmes, Stephanie Hedlund, Megan Murphy
Art Direction: Neil Klinepier

Library of Congress Cataloging-in-Publication Data

Wheeler, Jill C., 1964-
    Jessica Simpson / Jill C. Wheeler.
        p. cm. -- (Young profiles)
    Includes index.
    ISBN 1-59197-879-3
    1. Simpson, Jessica, 1980---Juvenile literature. 2. Singers--United States--Biography--
Juvenile literature. I. Title. II. Series.

ML3930.S57W54 2004
782.42164'092--dc22
[B]
                                                                    2004054454

Contents

Voice of an Angel 4

Profile of Jessica Simpson 6

Gospel Girl 8

Mickey Mouse Club 10

Amazing Grace 12

From Gospel to Pop 14

Moving Up 16

On the Road 18

Diva in Training 20

Ups and Downs 22

Irresistible 24

New Projects 26

Glossary 30

Web Sites 31

Index 32

Voice of an Angel

Jessica Simpson's voice has been compared to that of an angel. In 2004, Jessica was invited to be a VH1 Diva. She joined other powerhouse singers, such as Patti Labelle and Cyndi Lauper. The seventh annual VH1 "Divas" concert raised more than $300,000 to fund school music programs.

Jessica has brought a refreshing new attitude to pop music. Her songs of love and faith take advantage of her incredible **vocal** range. It spans an amazing five **octaves**! With each record, Jessica displays her growing talent.

So far, Jessica has had a successful career in music and television. Her first CD, *Sweet Kisses*, went double **platinum**. Her reality show, *Newlyweds: Nick and Jessica*, has been a popular show on MTV. Jessica has achieved fame without losing sight of her hometown values.

Jessica wowed the audience at VH1 "Divas" 2004 with two powerful solo performances.

Profile of Jessica Simpson

Name: Jessica Ann Simpson

Date of Birth: July 10, 1980

Place of Birth: Dallas, Texas

Current Home: San Fernando Valley, California

Height: Five feet, three inches

Parents: Joe and Tina Simpson

Sibling: Younger sister Ashlee

Husband: Nick Lachey, former 98 Degrees member

Job: Singer, songwriter, and television personality

Favorite Foods: Tex-Mex and fried food

Favorite Singer: Celine Dion

Favorite Song: "Take My Breath Away" by Berlin

Quote from Jessica: "I want people to fall in love with my voice before my image."

Gospel Girl

Jessica Ann Simpson was born on July 10, 1980, in Dallas, Texas. Her father, Joe, was a **psychologist** and a youth minister. Her mother, Tina, was a Sunday school teacher. Jessica has a younger sister, Ashlee.

As a child, Jessica loved to sing. She often roamed around the family's house singing along with the radio. One day, Joe decided to have her sing in church. It was the start of what would become a successful musical career.

Young Jessica soon began singing in the church choir. She also sang solos for the **congregation**. As a **gospel** singer, Jessica sang about faith. But, the songs were more than just words for her. Jessica grew up with a solid faith in God. She also had strong love for her family and her church community.

Opposite page: *Jessica's strong family values can be seen in her connection with her sister, Ashlee.*

Mickey Mouse Club

Jessica's singing career nearly ended when she was 12. She learned that the Disney Channel was **recruiting** performers for the *Mickey Mouse Club*. Disney sent the casting call to young people around the nation.

Jessica signed up for the regional **audition** in Dallas. She was one of about 30,000 young performers seeking a spot on the show. Jessica was chosen to advance in the competition. She went to Florida for a two-week audition. The audition included acting, **vocal**, and dance lessons.

The producers thought Jessica was perfect for the show. Yet, she recalls

Jessica auditioned for the Mickey Mouse Club *in 1992. Competitors Britney Spears* (front right), *Christina Aguilera* (second row, right), *and Justin Timberlake* (third row, right) *went on to become Mouseketeers.*

getting nervous as she watched the other contestants perform. She froze when her turn came. She forgot her dance moves and the words to her song.

Jessica definitely had talent. However, some of her competitors had more experience in front of a camera. When Jessica lost, she was ready to give up on a singing career.

Jessica's father, Joe, has been an inspiration to her throughout the years.

Jessica's family encouraged her to keep trying. Her father's faith in her led him to become her manager. Jessica realized music was important to her. She began taking voice lessons to improve her natural abilities.

Amazing Grace

It did not take long for Jessica to bounce back from her disappointment. Two years later, she was singing at a church camp. She performed "Amazing Grace" **a cappella**.

Buster Soaries was a guest speaker visiting the camp that night. He was launching a new **gospel** music label called Proclaim Records. He asked Jessica if she would work with Proclaim. Jessica eagerly signed on with the label when she was 14 years old.

For the next couple of years, Jessica was hard at work. She continued improving her voice and looking for new songs for her record. Jessica also attended J.J. Pearce High School in Richardson, Texas. There, she was head cheerleader and was even crowned homecoming queen twice.

Then in 1996, Proclaim Records went out of business. Despite all of her hard work, Jessica's CD was never released. Once again, she considered quitting the business.

Jessica's family did not let her give in to defeat. Her grandmother provided her with the money to finish the album. Jessica also began traveling the Christian Youth Conference circuit with her father. Joe preached, Jessica sang, and they sold copies of her CD.

Jessica's persistence eventually paid off. She now travels all over the United States, singing for people of all ages.

From Gospel to Pop

Jessica became quite successful on the **gospel** circuit. She performed with such gospel giants as CeCe Winans and Kirk Franklin. Sometimes the audiences numbered 20,000 people. Jessica and her family sold every copy of the CD they had made.

Jessica's gospel music career was going well. However, she knew she could sell more records if she crossed over to pop music. But, she wanted her career to remain in line with her personal values. Jessica wanted to be a positive role model.

Joe and Tina wanted to ease the transition from gospel to pop music. So, they hired a lawyer who specialized in the entertainment business. The lawyer arranged for Jessica to meet with nine different record labels.

In August 1997, Jessica met with Tommy Mottola of Sony Music Entertainment. Jessica recalls meeting with Mottola as the most nerve-racking experience of her life.

Jessica had planned to sing two songs for Mottola. However, he told her to stop after the first one. He offered her a record contract on the spot. Mottola also told her he admired her beliefs. He said Sony's record label Columbia would support her desire to perform within her values.

Jessica has said, "Faith has helped me to be a strong person and stay levelheaded. It brings me peace. In this business you definitely need peace."

Moving Up

Seventeen-year-old Jessica was thrilled. She felt very good about her decision to join Columbia. She began to work on her first pop album for the label.

Jessica was entering a very competitive market. Her former *Mickey Mouse Club* competitors Britney Spears and Christina Aguilera were well on their way to stardom. She and Columbia knew her work had to be different.

Mottola advised her to focus on recording ballads first. He wanted to make sure the album emphasized Jessica's incredible voice. Jessica was happy to comply. Her desire was to make music that would touch people of all ages. She also wanted her voice to be respected.

By this time, Jessica's busy schedule was interfering with her schooling. She was forced to take her classes by mail in her senior year. She received her general equivalency diploma (GED) in early 1998.

Jessica's busy schedule included television appearances on The Tonight Show with Jay Leno, Saturday Night Live, *and* That 70s Show.

On the Road

In December 1998, Jessica met 98 Degrees singer Nick Lachey. They both attended the Hollywood Christmas Parade in Los Angeles, California. Jessica liked Nick from the start. She went home and told her family that she had met the man she wanted to marry.

Busy schedules prevented Jessica and Nick from seeing each other again until January 1999. They began dating shortly after that. It was hard for them to stay in touch. Yet, they made it a policy to see each other every two weeks.

Jessica's dreams of pop stardom came true in 1999. That year, she began traveling the pop circuit to promote her upcoming CD. She landed a 42-date **gig** opening for 98 Degrees. This brought Jessica added fame.

Opposite page: *On Jessica's first album,* Sweet Kisses, *Jessica and Nick sang "Where You Are."*

Diva in Training

Jessica's first Columbia album, *Sweet Kisses*, arrived in stores late in 1999. The album featured soulful ballads and bouncy pop tunes. All of the songs showcased her amazing voice.

As she had hoped, *Sweet Kisses* appealed to more than just teens. Reviewers called Jessica a diva in training. They compared her abilities to stars such as Mariah Carey. **Critics** also commented on the passion evident in her ballads.

One of those ballads was "I Wanna Love You Forever." It was right in line with Jessica's old-fashioned, romantic side. Another popular song was "Woman in Me," which was sung with Destiny's Child. That song touched on the importance of self-esteem and self-worth.

Jessica was happy with her work on *Sweet Kisses*. So were her new pop fans. The album went **platinum** during her tour. Her song, "Did You Ever Love Somebody," landed on the sound track for *Dawson's Creek*.

Jessica and the members of Destiny's Child shared the same record label.

Ups and Downs

Following the 98 Degrees tour, Jessica opened for Ricky Martin. This time, she had her own **troupe** of dancers. They included her younger sister, Ashlee.

Touring helped Jessica sharpen her stage skills, although it was not always easy. In December 1999, she came down with a bad **respiratory** infection. Several shows had to be canceled while she underwent treatment.

There was one bright spot, however. While recovering, Jessica got a call from her idol, Celine Dion. Dion advised her to take it easy and get better soon.

Jessica also had her share of embarrassing moments onstage. Once, she opened for Ricky Martin in New York City. She bent down to hit a note and her pants split in the back.

Jessica raced offstage to her mom. She put her mother's jeans on and went back onstage. She then apologized to everyone and kept on singing. Jessica's ripped pants were later **auctioned** off for charity. They sold for $8,000.

Jessica's mother, Tina, helps her with her hair and wardrobe.

Irresistible

Jessica's second album, *Irresistible*, was released in 2001. Reviewers said *Irresistible* was more **sophisticated** than her first record. The new album showcased her **vocal** skills even more. The title track, "Irresistible," landed in the top ten on *Billboard*'s Top 40 Tracks.

Jessica also proved to be irresistible to Nick. He proposed to her on a yacht off the coast of Hawaii in February 2002. The couple married that October. Then they moved to their new home near Los Angeles, California.

In 2003, the couple's home became the set of a reality television show for MTV. *Newlyweds: Nick and Jessica* showed how the couple was adjusting to married life.

The show had many funny moments. In one, cameras caught Jessica returning home from a tour. She found 20 loads of laundry waiting for her. She got angry and started throwing the laundry off the bedroom balcony.

Jessica and Nick

New Projects

*N*ewlyweds helped Jessica receive the attention that she needed when she released her third CD. This CD was titled *In This Skin*. Jessica felt that this was her most honest work.

Jessica received a gold record for In This Skin.

In This Skin also marked the start of songwriting for Jessica. She says Nick inspired many of the songs she wrote for the record. She admits, "He is the reason why I write about love." The couple hopes to record an album together one day.

Meanwhile, Jessica has stayed busy with many different projects. She helped create a book about wedding planning. It is based on her experience planning her wedding.

Jessica's repeated success is allowing her to grow more **confident** in herself. She says, "I am more ready than I've ever been. It's a beautiful thing this time around. For the first time, I really have something to give and the power to impact."

In April 2004, Jessica released a new line of beauty products called Dessert. She also hopes to expand her acting career. She would eventually like to combine singing with acting. Anything Jessica attempts is sure to be a success.

Jessica Simpson

Glossary

a cappella - without musical accompaniment.

auction - a public sale at which goods are sold to the highest bidder.

audition - a short performance to test someone's ability.

confident - to be sure of one's self.

congregation - a number of people assembled together, often for worship or religious instruction.

critic - a professional who gives his or her opinion on art or performances.

gig - a booking for a musician to play in public.

gospel - the message of a religious teacher. Gospel music is related to the teachings of Jesus.

octave - the eight-note gap in a musical scale between a note and the next note of the same name.

platinum - a term describing an album that has sold more than 1 million copies.

psychologist - a person who specializes in studying the mind and the reasons for thoughts and behavior.

recruit - to get someone to join a group. A person who is recruited is also called a recruit.

respiratory - having to do with the system of organs involved with breathing.

sophisticated - having worldly knowledge or experience.

troupe - a group of dancers or actors that travels.

vocal - related to the voice.

30

Web Sites

To learn more about Jessica Simpson, visit ABDO Publishing Company on the World Wide Web at **www.abdopub.com**. Web sites about Jessica are featured on our Book Links page. These links are routinely monitored and updated to provide the most current information available.

Index

A

Aguilera, Christina 16

C

Carey, Mariah 20
Christian Youth
    Conference 13, 14

D

Dallas, Texas 8, 10
Dawson's Creek 20
Dessert 27
Destiny's Child 20
Dion, Celine 22
Disney Channel 10

E

education 12, 16

F

family 8, 11, 13, 14,
    18, 22
Florida 10
Franklin, Kirk 14

H

Hawaii 24

I

In This Skin 26
Irresistible 24

L

Labelle, Patti 4
Lachey, Nick 18, 24, 26
Lauper, Cyndi 4
Los Angeles, California
    18, 24

M

Martin, Ricky 22
Mickey Mouse Club 10,
    11, 16
Mottola, Tommy 14,
    15, 16
MTV 4, 24

N

New York City, New
    York 22

*Newlyweds: Nick and
    Jessica* 4, 24, 26
98 Degrees 18, 22

R

record labels 12, 14,
    15, 16, 20
Richardson, Texas 12

S

Soaries, Buster 12
Spears, Britney 16
Sweet Kisses 4, 20, 24

T

touring 13, 14, 18, 20,
    22, 24

V

VH1 4

W

Winans, CeCe 14